Decluttering Your Marriage

Decluttering Your Marriage

Douglas Wilson

Moscow, Idaho

Douglas Wilson, *Decluttering Your Marriage*
Copyright ©2017 by Douglas Wilson

Published by Canon Press
P. O. Box 8729, Moscow, Idaho 83843
800-488-2034 | www.canonpress.com

Cover illustration by Forrest Dickison
Cover design by James Engerbretson
Interior design by Valerie Anne Bost

Unless otherwise indicated, all Scripture quotations are from the King James Version.

All rights reserved. No part of this publication may be reproduced, stored in a retrieval system, or transmitted in any form by any means, electronic, mechanical, photocopy, recording, or otherwise, without prior permission of the author, except as provided by USA copyright law.

Table of Contents

1. Marriage and the Clutter of Sin // 7
2. Practical Tips for Confession of Sin // 25
3. Decluttering Your Marriage Checklist // 39

PART 1

Marriage and the Clutter of Sin

Brethren, if a man be overtaken in a fault, ye which are spiritual restore such an one in the spirit of meekness; considering thyself, lest thou also be tempted.

GALATIANS 6:1

Since this short book you are reading is about marriage, you may be wondering why I begin with a passage in which marriage is not even mentioned. However, though marriage is not mentioned here, sin is, and sin is the preeminent destructive force within marriage. People like to explain a marriage's failure by pointing to non-ethical factors like personal incompatibility, but according to the Bible, marriage is fundamentally a matter of obedience and disobedience.

On Sunday at church, it is very easy to be a Christian. You are surrounded by people who are praising the Lord and saying things that are edifying. What is so hard about that? All you have to do is go to church once a week, put up with that for an hour and a half, and then get out. But on Monday morning, you are dealing with people who will not put their socks in a place that can be located later and who expect you to know where they are and, not only that, they have been doing this for twenty years. As you continue to get exasperated at similar various day-to-day problems, you need to consider carefully how to handle this sort of thing.

A marriage that is several decades old can grow to be wonderful, like aging wine, but it can also grow seriously unwonderful. Marriage is the best thing on earth, and marriage is the worst thing on earth. It is the best thing if you are walking under the blessing of God, but it is the worst hypocrisy, the worst stench, the worst exasperation, if it is not under the blessing of God. Marriage under the blessing of God is God's greatest earthly gift, though it is not His only gift. It is not true that if you are unmarried, God is saying, "Sorry, no gifts for you." God has gifts for people in every station of life, but we have to rank the gift of marriage right at the top, provided it is under the blessing of God.

If it is not under the blessing of God, then a person who has not received that gift has been blessed by not being in that condition. It is foolish to envy people who struggle with something. If someone is not married, then they do lack a blessing that some people have, but they also lack exasperations that those people have. (It is remarkable how unselfish you can be in an apartment all by yourself.) Of course, marriage in one sense changes who you are in certain ways, but it also simply amplifies what you are. Many people think that when they got married, they turned into selfish people. What actually happened is they plugged the guitar into the amp and turned it up to eleven, and the selfish tune they had been playing the whole time suddenly became audible.

Marriage is a good thing or a bad thing depending on whether it is under the blessing of God. God's best gifts are the worst things in the world once they have been corrupted. Satan fell from the highest height and consequently is the worst devil. When a marriage crashes or is polluted, it becomes the most destructive thing in the world, and can mess everything up.

THE DAUNTING PILE

Marriages can get badly cluttered, like a neglected garage, attic, or basement, and when things get cluttered, people do not really know what to do about the clutter. There is such a big pile that they do not know where to begin. If you have a cluttered garage, you might one day resolve to set aside a Saturday to go out to the garage and work at it all day. Then, when you go out first thing in the morning and open the garage door, all you can do is look at the pile, stare at it for five minutes, and then close the door and go back inside and pray for a fire. However, to start fixing the problem, you do not need to know anything about what is at the bottom of the pile. The only thing you need to know about is what you can see on top of the pile that you put there last week. Similarly, when you are dealing with clutter in your marriage, you need to deal with the things you know about.

The old reprobate, Mark Twain, once said, "It ain't those parts of the Bible that I can't understand that bother me; it's the parts that I do understand." The things that trip us up are the parts of the Bible about humbling ourselves, seeking forgiveness, and putting things right. These texts are perfectly understandable, so we retreat to obscure texts and theological issues. In John 4, while talking with Jesus, the Samaritan woman deflected the conversation from the real issue: "Hmmm. You have brought up an interesting point about my personal life, but should we worship on this mountain or on the other one?" And Jesus, having a completely different agenda for the conversation, pointed out, "You have had five husbands, and the one you are with now is not your husband."

Ambrose Bierce was a very learned and witty reprobate, but we ought to take his definition of a Christian in The Devil's Dictionary to heart: "Christian, noun. One who believes that the New Testament is a divinely inspired book admirably suited to the spiritual needs of his neighbor. One who follows the teachings of Christ so long as they are not inconsistent with a life of sin."* Need we say more?

"YE WHICH ARE SPIRITUAL"

Galatians 6:1 lays down some important principles for the process of decluttering any relationship, but particularly the relationship with one's spouse.

Before we go further, if you picked up this book thinking, "At last! Help for dealing with my spouse's sins! Here,

---

* *The Unabridged Devil's Dictionary*, ed. David E. Schultz and S.J. Joshi (Athens, GA: University of Georgia Press, 2000), 35 [Christian, n.].

dear, come and look at this!" then this book will not do you any good.

Galatians 6:1 says that if you see some other person has a problem, you have instructions on what to do. Seeing their fault is not necessarily wrong; they might really have a problem, and you might really see it. As Jesus says in Matthew 18, if your brother has wronged you, you may go and show him his fault. The Bible does not require us to be blind to the sins that others commit against us or to always assume that we are at fault. But the Bible does require us to consider whether we might be involved.

So if someone is overtaken in a fault, who should correct the fault? Paul first states what the qualifications are for the one undertaking the job of correcting another person. Correcting someone else is a high and scary office, and we should think about it in the same way we think about jumping out of an airplane: such a thing is dangerous and fraught with peril. Paul says the task is limited to those "which are spiritual." This is the first bar. If someone is spiritual, then he is qualified, but if he is annoyed, bothered, irritated, angry, upset, ruffled, or any other synonym for those that you can find on thesaurus.com, then he is the one person on the planet who is disqualified from saying anything whatsoever about that person's sin.

Paul assumes that the brother really might be overtaken in a trespass and that he really might require correction, but he still says, "Ye which are spiritual restore such a one." The problem is that when you are qualified to correct someone, you are not motivated. If everything is joy and sunshine and you see someone sin, you might be tempted to think, "Why would I correct anybody now? They may be sinning, but that's no skin off my nose, because I'm not irritated." Oftentimes our moral policing of other people has nothing to do with our convenience or our concern about how they are doing. If you are correcting someone, it ought to be motivated by concern for them and ultimately by love. Instead, however, it is often driven by simple selfishness.

Moving away from marriage, imagine that your kids are careening around the living room. You can correct them, because you want them to grow up to be disciplined people who have respect for property and do not destroy things. If this is the case, you are correcting them for their sake. Or you might snap at them because you have got one nerve left and they are on it. You did not do that for them. You did that for you. In that case, you are not teaching your children to refrain from careening around the living room. You are teaching them how to be selfish. You think you are teaching modesty and decorum in their deportment in the living room, but what you are actually teaching them is how to snap at their kids.

Turning to the marriage relationship, if a husband is snapping at his wife, or a wife is nagging her husband, then they are not qualified to correct one another. If you are annoyed, bothered, frustrated, exasperated, and so on, then keep your mouth shut—you are not qualified. You may sputter to yourself, "But look what they're doing! It's crucial that they get corrected!" However, if it is crucial that they get corrected, then it is also crucial that you deal with your own sin first!

Paul says that if a brother is overtaken in a fault, the only ones who may correct are those who are spiritual. If you are spiritual, then you now can listen to the rest of the instructions. When you are qualified, you are not motivated; and when you are motivated by your annoyance and anger and irritation to correct someone, you are not qualified. Put a lid on it. Do not do anything. Bite your tongue. And biting your tongue involves more than looking like a storm cloud in the corner, when you need to be humble and contrite and interested in how the other person is faring.

"RESTORE SUCH A ONE"

Suppose, however, that someone is overtaken in a trespass, and suppose further that you are qualified to say something. You do not have a dog in the fight, and you are not personally irritated or annoyed. Even then Paul adds additional cautions. The first is that you are there to administer a restoration, not a beatdown. "Ye who are spiritual restore such a one." You're not there to score points. In many marriages where things are not good, behind the scenes the husband and wife are keeping accounts against one another.

1 Corinthians 13 says that love does not keep a record of wrongs. I was reading a marriage book years ago, and the author said one time a woman came in and plopped a scrapbook on his desk and said something like, "There! That's everything my husband has done wrong for twenty-three years!" What kind of spirit does that reveal? Whatever it reveals, it is not love.

Love does not keep a record of wrongs. If you have a record and then you go to correct the person, you will not only be correcting that person for their most recent offense, but you will also be saying in the back of your mind, "And this also vindicates everything I said in our argument three weeks ago on this same topic!" If you are doing that, you are not coming for restoration.

You may have watched a city league softball game where one side demolishes the other team. At a certain point in the game, the losing team stops competing with the other team and starts competing with itself. The players begin to blame and find fault with each other, and as soon as that happens, it's all over. Everybody is on the same team, and it is simply devouring itself. Husbands, for instance, can be competitive, and sometimes they may feel like they just scored one on their wife. In reality he just dunked the basketball in his own hoop. You are not winning when someone on your team loses. God established a man and a woman to be a unit, a team that operates together, and if someone is more concerned about vindicating themselves, then they have got things so muddled and upside down that it is hard to know where to begin.

"IN A SPIRIT OF MEEKNESS"

So the first qualification for you who are spiritual is that you are there to administer restoration, not a beatdown. The second qualification is that you must conduct yourself in a spirit of meekness, gentleness, and humility. "Brethren, if a man be overtaken in a fault, ye which are spiritual restore such a one in the spirit of meekness." If you come across like a buzz-saw or an accuser or you say "You always...! You never...!" then you have two problems. First, it is not true, and second, it is a spirit of accusation. You are being a devil within your family when you say, "You always do this!" or "You never do that!" or "Why are you always so offensive?" If you want to know why people are defensive when they are talking to you, it might be because you are an accuser.

"CONSIDERING THYSELF, LEST THOU ALSO BE TEMPTED"

The third requirement is that you must keep one eye on yourself, "considering thyself, lest thou also be tempted." You must remember that you too are susceptible to temptation.

You cannot have a cluttered marriage without somebody sinning, and it usually includes both parties. Even if someone else has sinned, you may have sinned too and can only help if you get yourself squared away first. If you already succumbed to temptation, or if you already have that edge in your voice, you need to stay out of it.

If you are married and staying out of it is not an option, then you need to confess your sins right away and deal with yourself first. Otherwise, if you cannot come with restoration in your heart, stay out of it. If you are not functioning in a spirit of meekness, then stay out of it. If you are not mindful of your own frailty in these things on this issue, then stay out of it. Surrender to God. Drop your pride. Let it go.

THE BIGGEST ROADBLOCK

I hesitate to write this, but after approximately four decades of marriage counseling, I have pretty much seen it all. I have seen astonishing levels of denseness, and I have seen people who are simply unwilling to consider even the possibility that they might be contributing to their own mess. What creates intractable marriage problems? The answer to that is not sins, but rather one sin—the sin of pride. The one thing a person who is proud cannot do is go to another person in a spirit of meekness.

I do not want to make light of any particular sin, because all sin is destructive, but not all sins are equally deceptive. Imagine a husband comes back from a trip having purchased something that the family cannot afford and, having purchased it, he realizes that he was being stupid. Imagine a wife comes back from the mall having purchased something, and the husband says, "But honey, we decided we weren't able to do this." Usually, the person who did it recognizes his fault instantly and says, "Yes, you're right. We did decide that. I wasn't thinking. I was wrong. Would you please forgive me?" Now that is a sin, and it is a problem that sows distrust, and I do not want to minimize it, but pastorally speaking, it is not the snake-pit that the intractable problems are.

When a husband busts himself over pornography or anger or financial irresponsibility, though it is a sin and it is problematic and difficult, pastorally speaking, at least it has handles. The person may have sinned, but he has also acknowledged his sin, so there is something to work with here. The thing that is nearly impossible to work with is the primal sin, the sin of pride. With other sins, things can be messy, but pretty straightforward.

"Be not righteous over much; neither make thyself over wise: why shouldest thou destroy thyself?" (Eccl. 7:16). Now obviously being super spiritual is not spiritual at all. Nonetheless, you can destroy your marriage with what you think are your virtues. If someone drinks too much, they can repent of that, because it is easy to identify. However, many Christians are marital Pharisees, flatly convinced of their own righteousness and of the ungrateful unrighteousness of everyone else, and they are exasperated with the obtuseness of the counselor who fails to recognize the evil that they (the righteous one) must deal with daily.

This is a common problem in the church, and it is a common problem in conservative, evangelical, Bible-believing, Reformed churches. In the story of the Pharisee and the publican who both went down to the Temple to pray, the loser went into the temple and said, "God be merciful to me a sinner," while the Pharisee said, "God, I thank thee, that I am not as other men are, extortioners, unjust, adulterers, or even as this publican. I fast twice in the week, I give tithes of all that I possess" (Lk. 18:13, 11–12). Let us change that into Reformed theological language, shall we? What do modern Pharisees say? "Soli Deo Gloria! To God alone be the glory for how wonderful I am. To God alone be the glory for how right I am!" Jesus says the Pharisee was the one who went home unjustified. The one who quoted one of the solas went home unjustified, and the one who is just a mess went home justified.

This is a common and very easy sin for Christians to commit. If I could resort to the old evangelical cliche, some people miss heaven by eighteen inches, the distance between the head and the heart. They have unhappy marriages, all because they missed it by eighteen inches. They have read the marriage books and heard the marriage sermons, and they like the doctrine of headship and submission. They like the way it all looks in the blueprints and in the abstract, but then they say, "It would look that way in my house if it weren't for all these other sinners who are always messing things up!"

This is a common problem for people who know what they believe, read their Bibles, and have their doctrine squared away. This is why Jesus thought it was necessary to go around saying what would have seemed simply crazy at the time. Matthew 21:31: "Verily I say unto you, that the publicans and the harlots go into the kingdom of God before you!"

Around this time, there were about six thousand Pharisees total in Israel. They were not priests like the Sadducees. These were basically successful businessmen and merchants who had decided to have high standards of holiness and separation. In fact the root for the word "Pharisee" is very similar to the root for the word "Puritan," and both movements had similar points of origin. I think that Ezra was probably the first Pharisee, and that the movement had a noble origin. By the time Jesus came on the scene, the Pharisees were the most highly respected group in mainstream Israel and they had a good reputation that Jesus destroyed for all time. He basically told all the assembled conference speakers of Israel, "The hookers and the crack addicts are getting into heaven before you guys." Why is he saying this? Because the far greater temptation to the human heart is the crack cocaine of self-congratulation, and the addiction of always being the hero of whatever story you are in.

Look at some crowd of people going down the street: every last person on that street is the protagonist in their very own movie, and some of them even have earbuds with the soundtrack going the whole time. In their version of the story, in every encounter, in every interaction, they are the good guy or protagonist, and everyone else is the antagonist or the villain. How can there be so many heroes of so many stories, when everything is so messed up? The only way that can be the case is if most of the people are wrong.

This self-congratulatory patting yourself on the back is something that we must deal with, especially in our marriages. You call it righteous indignation, but God calls it the wrath of man. You call it maternal concern, but God calls it manipulative worry. You call it prudent input, but God calls it a critical spirit. You call it decisive leadership (perhaps coupled with gigantic faith), but God calls it financial irresponsibility. You call it theological precision, but God calls it neglecting the weightier matters of the law. You call it precision, but God calls it tithing out of the spice rack.

Who repents of righteous indignation? Who repents of maternal concern, prudent input, decisive leadership, or theological precision? Nobody. This is why many pastors who are dealing with marriage problems often wish there was the counseling equivalent of a SWAT team that could be called in to wake people up and make them see that the real reason they are at loggerheads is because they are not loving one another.

Oliver Cromwell in one of his pleas to the Scots says, "I beseech ye in the bowels of Christ to consider that ye might be mistaken." One author says that this is a characteristic that has not been bequeathed to Scots as of yet.

COMMUNICATION

You might be a player, and oftentimes in marriage disasters, the player need not be very active. If you know where all the buttons are, it is amazing how you can push them all without moving very much. You can push your wife's or your husband's buttons by just moving your eyebrows or by the tone of your voice. We all like to play dumb about our own role. If you take a simple sentence like, "We're having lasagna tonight," all you have to do is to italicize different words to completely transform the meaning of the words: "*We're* having lasagna tonight?" "We're having *lasagna* tonight?" "We're having lasagna?" We then excuse ourselves by saying, "All I said was, 'We're having lasagna tonight,' and she went off like a volcano!" When a wife blows up at something her husband said at the end of a long day, the husband retreats and pleads the dictionary: "All I said was 'We're. Having. Lasagna. Tonight.' Look up every individual word in the dictionary. Not one of them is objectionable!" Nothing whatever is objectionable about that sentence, because eye-rolls and tones of voice are not in the dictionary. In these encounters, the only person's face you cannot see is your own.

So consider that you might possibly be mistaken and that you might be a part of the problem. We do not know how we come across to other people, and a good part of how we come across should be calculated from how people respond to us, without blaming them for the response. There are times where you can grow and get to the point where you can tell if someone else is falsely attacking how you come across, but the possibility that you might be part of the problem has never occurred to you that you are not qualified to go and correct somebody else.

Suppose a husband comes home and things are cool and quiet, and he says, "Honey, is anything wrong?" If she says, "No, nothing's wrong," then he might say, "Good! For a second I thought something was wrong," and go to watch the news. When he asks about dinner two hours later, and there is a huge meltdown, he will then say, "I specifically asked if something was wrong, and you said nothing was wrong!" However, if she were out with her girlfriends and someone said, "Is something wrong?" and she said, "No, nothing's wrong," her friend would say, "Oh, you poor dear! Tell me all about it!" A guy watching this would say, "What just happened? When I have a conversation, I need antecedents!" When she says, "No," in this context, it actually means, "There are so many things wrong that I cannot put my finger on any one thing! Besides, any idiot could see that something was wrong, and you come in asking me questions just to annoy me!"

In a snarl like this, neither of them sees the folly of what they are doing. You cannot talk the way you talk to your husband or wife in the same way you talk to the mirror. You do not see yourself. You do not understand yourself, and you must look in the mirror of God's Word, as James tells us. Look in the mirror of the Word, and the Word tells you that the odds are pretty good that you are contributing to this misunderstanding far more than you know.

Therefore, if you are at an impasse in your relationship, then you need to recognize that your pile of clutter is almost certainly the result of two piles of clutter that have merged. If you come to the realization that you have a significant amount of unconfessed sin in your life, then do not start with the other person's problems. If they need to see how easy it is to put things right, show them how. Astonish the world.

Proverbs 28:13 says, "He that covereth his sins shall not prosper, but whoso confesseth and forsaketh them shall have mercy." Why is your marriage not prospering? The reasons many marriages are cluttered is because many people are covering sins with something other than the blood of Jesus. People cover sins with their own evasions, excuses, rationalizations, and pride, and none of that can deal with sin. Only the blood of Jesus can deal with sin. As 1 John 1:9 says, "If we confess our sins, He is faithful and just to forgive us our sins and to cleanse us from all unrighteousness."

A THIRD PARTY

Moralism does not work in marriage any better than it works anywhere else. High standards and traditional values are the ropes that sinners use to throttle one another. A home that is spiritual is a home that overflows with grace, and a spiritual marriage is a marriage that overflows with grace. You cannot overflow with Jesus and not be overflowing with grace, and it is not possible for a marriage to be overflowing with grace unless it is overflowing with Christ. And by Christ I do not mean a distant Christ or a deistic God on a far mountain that gives us commands so that we can condemn one another.

As Psalm 130:3 says, if God were to mark iniquities, who could stand? We need justification. We need forgiveness. We need grace. We need Christ, and that means if we have received Christ, we will also extend Christ to others. If you are not extending Christ, then you are trying to get people to believe that you have not received Christ. You forgive because you have been forgiven. You extend grace the way you have received grace, and how much grace you extend is a measure of how much grace you think you have received.

So Christ must be present in order for a marriage to be blessed. There is no such thing as a Christless, blessed marriage. Christ need not be present for entropy to govern everything. He need not be present for your attic to be filled with useless clutter. He need not be present for pride to take over the atmosphere of the dinner table. He need not be present for conversations to grow snark and criticism the way gardens grow thistles all by themselves. But He must be present for us to see all these things rightly as thistles. He must be present in order for us to be able to dig them up to pull them out. In order for grace to be there, He must be there. It is not possible for Him to be there apart from the Word; apart from the Gospel; apart from Him crucified, buried, resurrected; and apart from the Spirit who takes that Gospel and applies it to individuals, enabling sinners—two sinners, one man and one woman—to live together in harmony. All of this is only possible in the gospel.

PART 2

PRACTICAL TIPS FOR CONFESSION OF SIN

He that covereth his sins shall not prosper: but whoso confesseth and forsaketh them shall have mercy.

PROVERBS 28:13

In the first part of this book, I addressed the problem of how pride and how a lack of self-reflection compounds the problem of cluttered relationships. In this part I am going to focus on some practical steps that will help you get things picked up and then help you keep it picked up. If you were contemplating moving to the Swiss Alps to start your own signature ministry, you could call it Debris!

PROCRASTINATION

Proverbs 28:13 not only contains overt teaching about confession of sin and the blessing of God, but also contains an unstated assumption about time which we can make explicit in a paraphrase: "He who covers his sins for any length of time shall not prosper for that length of time, but whoever confesses and forsakes them immediately shall have mercy immediately." In other words, there is a "now" implied in the text.

This is one of the things that you might think goes without saying, and it does go without saying when the prideful heart of man is not messing with us and getting in the way. When it comes to confessing sin and humbling ourselves, there is always an argument for later: "Well, they're not in the best mood to receive it right now." "I think I need to go to church and get some spiritual resources first." "I'll do it tonight when I go to bed." "I'll do it Sunday before the confession of sin." Later, later, later.

When it comes to humbling yourself, there is always an argument for later. The devil is always going to be at your elbow, suggesting some other time than now. This is why it says in Psalm 95:7-8, "To day if ye will hear his voice, harden not your heart." God tells us to repent now, while the devil says, "If it must be addressed—and we're not quite sure about that—why not tomorrow? Why not sleep on it? Why not meditate on it?"

We do it right away whenever what we need to do does not involve humbling ourselves. Suppose you burned yourself, and a doctor gave you some ointment for the burn and told you to put it on. Would you ask whether he meant for you to put it on in August? Obviously not. If you just got burned and it hurts enough, you might ask questions about how often to put it on, but you would put it on right away.

If you stop covering up your sins now, you will also receive the promised blessing of the prosperity of God now. Since that prosperity is defined according to the Word, not according to our own imaginations, we must do what He says we must do in order to receive it, and that means we must confess now.

THE NECESSITY OF COVERING

It is not a bad impulse to want to cover sins. They are genuinely shameful, and they cry out for a covering. Our own lame efforts to cover them with lies, bluster, and moralistic furniture polish are not wrong because they cover, but rather because they do not cover.

Every sinner should want his sins to be covered, but the only thing that really covers sin is not shifts and evasions, but the blood of our great high priest, Jesus Christ. Every other way of dealing with sin has to be done over and over again, and the fact that you have to keep doing it shows that it does not work. If you confess your sin and receive forgiveness from God for that sin, you are cleansed. It is done. If you did not sin at all, you do not have to worry about it, and if you are forgiven, you do not have to worry about it either. If someone asked you something and you tell them the truth, you do not spend all day trying to persuade yourself that it was really okay that you told them the truth.

You do not have to rationalize telling the truth; you have to rationalize the lie. If you keep trying to cover, over and over and over again, then it's not really covering. It is as if you have a little cloth that is three square feet and you are trying to cover a couple of acres with it. You keep moving the cloth, trying to see if you can cover everything.

Again, the problem is not with wanting it to be covered. The problem is with you wanting to do the covering. Like the woman with the discharge of blood in the gospels, the more the doctors treated her, the worse it got. Knowing the need for the covering is not the problem. Jesus Christ covers sin, and if you are put right with God, you are put right with God at every level and in every respect.

Everyone who is truly converted is justified as though they had never sinned. When God looks at you, He looks at the righteousness of Jesus Christ. When God considers your legal standing before Him, He sees nothing other than the perfections of Jesus Christ.

And then, having given you the legal standing of the justified righteousness of Jesus Christ, He is free to get to work on what's actually going on in your day-to-day life where there are remaining sins that have to be addressed, confessed, and forgiven. However, as you address those remaining sins, your salvation and your standing before God are not at stake. Only sin is at stake: God has to deal with that. Decluttering your marriage is simply an exercise in growing in sanctification.

If you are a child of God at all, you are forgiven, period, for anything you have done, for anything you are doing right now, and for anything you ever will do. To be justified in Jesus Christ means that His righteousness is imputed to you, and that all of your sins and everything you have ever done wrong was imputed to Him on the cross.

Now, with regard to your day-to-day sanctification and your interactions with others, there are many things that need to be addressed, improved, cleansed, and forgiven, but your standing with God is not at risk. Even when God admonishes or disciplines you, keep in mind the radical distinction between justification and sanctification. We should not set them at odds with each other—sanctification rides on the back of justification—but what God is doing with your sins now is only possible because of what He has already done for you in justification.

A TALE OF TWO HOUSES

Imagine two families living side-by-side. The dads work at the same company, the moms drive the same kind of minivan, and they have the same number of kids. The only visible difference between the homes is that one is apparently spotless, and the other is knee-deep in clutter. Life happens in both houses: they have similar activities, similar "parks and recs" events, similar in-and-out of the driveway stuff, similar yard work, similar mowing, similar laundry, similar meals.

The difference between the homes is not the rate at which things get dirty. The difference between the homes is the rate at which things get cleaned again. If you look at a Christian who is in the joy of the Lord as compared to one who is miserable, the difference is not that there is no sin in the life of the joyful one, but that there is no sin there now. The clean house has no breakfast bowls mounded on the breakfast table, but it's not because nobody eats breakfast there. They all had breakfast, they all used bowls, and they all opened the fridge just like in the other house. But in the clean house, they pick it up, put it away, rinse it out, and put it in the dishwasher right away. The difference between the homes is that last step.

When a young person sees an older Christian whom they respect, they often think that the person is so godly they have not sinned since 1978, when in reality the person is a sinner like everybody else. But what they do differently is they know to deal with it now.

When sin accumulates to a certain point in the home, you get Mama drama, where everything just blows. (Incidentally, Mama drama is just as often caused by dads and kids.) When it all blows, often a few little things are picked up and addressed, but the fundamental clutter remains.

The issue is not the rate at which things get dirty. Marriages will always include bumps, fusses, misunderstandings, and problems. However, when these problems arise, you will either push them away or you are going to deal with them right away. When you do not deal with them right away, they accumulate. Marriages that are put together are marriages where sin is not allowed to accumulate.

The Bible tells us to confess our faults, one to another (Jas. 5:16). This is something that should characterize life generally, but it is most obvious in the home. When people refuse to confess their faults to one another, it is glaringly obvious. If something just spilled, wipe it up now. If something just got knocked over, pick it up now. If something just got dirty, rinse it out and put it in the dishwasher now. It's simple to understand it, but it is often difficult to do.

CONFESSING OTHER PEOPLE'S SINS

Suppose one day your nine-year-old boy discovers that he can eat peas with his knife, and you bite his head off at the dinner table. You might defend yourself by saying that we need to deal with faults right away, and since eating peas with a knife is a fault, you dealt with it right away. But why is it wrong to eat peas with a knife in the first place? It's wrong because it's bad manners, as is biting off your son's head at the dinner table. Which is worse? The Bible tells us it would be far better to live in a house with a dry morsel where there is peace and harmony than to dwell in a house with multi-course dinners accompanied by disharmony and strife (Prov. 17:1). You do not want to live in a house that has all the externals but where there is strife at the center. Manners, rightly understood, are showing love in trifles, not a means of finding fault with one another.

There is a story of a high tone dinner to which an unlettered rube was invited. The unmannered guest saw a little finger bowl and drank from it. Everybody at the table gasped and looked at the host. In response, the host picked up his finger bowl and drank it. That is what good manners look like, because it's loving other people in trifles. It is not fault-finding or making up extra rules to attack people with. Spurgeon once said, "Faults are thick where love is thin." Oftentimes we use our standards so that we can justify not loving other people.

When you confess your sins, you must not try to confess theirs at the same time. If you confess your own sin to prime the pump of your husband's or wife's confession, you will be disappointed when they do not take the hint. If your husband or wife just says, "Thank you, you're forgiven," you will be angry and disappointed.

If you wrap up a barbed accusation in the thin, filmy gauze of a confession, that is not confession of sin either. "I'm sorry for being mildly annoyed at your egregious behavior just now." Here is a rule of thumb: when you confess a sin, confess as though you are the only person in the history of the world who ever did anything wrong; that is a true confession.

Even though you know that the other person theologically, practically, and historically has sinned as well, you must surrender your own ego in confession, and you do it by assuming that you are the only one at fault. Your emotions need the practice of confessing as though the other person were perfect.

KEEPING SHORT ACCOUNTS

If you were to ask me for the single most important bit of advice on marriage, it would be this: keep short accounts. By this, I simply mean dealing with it right away.

If you confess sin as you go, nothing is ever going to accumulate. If you have thirty years of accumulation, some big crisis will erupt, and you will not be able to meet it together, because you have a pile of grievances against each other. When you are laid off at work or there is a big health crisis or someone in the family dies, you will not be able to deal with it in a godly way because you are not functioning as a team.

If you are picking it up now, there is no problem that can hit your marriage that you will not be in a position to address. Conversely, if you refuse to deal with this accumulated pile, there is no problem so trivial that it cannot be the last straw that finally upends the whole thing. If you are in harmony and fellowship with one another, you can face great trials together, shoulder to shoulder. If you are not on the same team, at some point there is going to be some last-straw incident, such as the husband leaving his sock on the back of the couch. A sock is very trivial, but on the top of a mountain of grievances, it is not trivial at all.

When you get out of fellowship with one another, there are some helpful things to do to keep short accounts. By getting out of fellowship, I do not mean having a difference of opinion; those arise frequently and are not in themselves a problem. I am talking about when you are cranked, annoyed, irritated, bent, frosted, angry, ruffled, or agitated. If you do not like the shape of the other person's head, something is wrong.

What follows are a few rules of thumb for relationships. These rules are not laws from Mount Sinai, but merely basic house rules which Nancy and I agreed upon when we first got married. These are simply helpful reminders for dealing with sin now.

DO NOT SEPARATE WHILE OUT OF FELLOWSHIP

First, when you have had a bump, do not separate; stay together until it is fixed. The husband does not go to work and the wife does not leave to go shopping. When you have had a bump, you must pick it up now, and it must be addressed together, so do not separate. You dropped it together, you messed up together, you sinned together, so you need to stay together until it has been addressed.

How long does it take to get out of fellowship? Nanoseconds. You can be walking along thinking you are having a great day, and all of a sudden—blam!—and you're in sin. How long does it take to get out of fellowship? No time at all. How long does it take to get back in fellowship? "Oh weeks!" you will say. No, weeks is not getting back in fellowship. Weeks is calming down. Weeks is getting used to the clutter.

You can get back in fellowship in the same amount of time as it took you to get out of it. You can flare up and have a display of temper in a second, and you can humble yourself in a second. If you cannot humble yourself in a second, then you need to go talk to Jesus until you can humble yourself in a second. Even if bumps happen every day of the week right before you go to work, you need to confess right away. I am not saying you should be late for work, but rather that you should learn to humble yourself quickly.

If you have a bump before you are about to get into the car and go to work, fix it, apologize, humble yourself, and then go. Now, this does not mean everything needs to be figured out all at once. Say the bump was about the checkbook or finances. This does not mean that you cannot separate until you go down to the bank and get all the practical stuff sorted out. Rather, I am saying you cannot separate until the animus, the annoyance, the irritation, and the upsetness is gone. "Would you please forgive me for my grumpy attitude?" "Yes. Would you please forgive me for my impatient attitude?" "Yes." Pray, kiss, go. That should not burn a lot of daylight.

NO NEIGHBORS WHILE OUT OF FELLOWSHIP

Second, when you have had a bump, do not let anybody come in your home. Nobody. If the doorbell rings right after you have a bump, fix it quickly, but do not let them in until you are in fellowship.

If you have ever had a physically cluttered living room and then someone rings the doorbell, what happens on the way to the door? Whoosh! Everything is being picked up on the way. Your spiritual life is like that living room. Pick it up on the way to the door if you must, but the door does not open and they do not come into your house until it is clean. If they ring the doorbell twice and it's raining, then humble yourself quickly. Nobody gets to see you when you are out of fellowship with each other.

NO VISITING OUT OF FELLOWSHIP

Third, when you have had a bump, do not go into anybody else's home. Suppose you are newlyweds and you are going to a Bible study and you have a bump in the car on the way (science has shown that 80% of all marital bumps happen in the car). Fix it, and do not spend 45 minutes out by the curb fixing it while people peer through the blinds wondering what you're doing. Humble yourself and then go in. Pick it up now, and other people will not see you disheveled. Everybody has laundry, but you should not let it pile up on the front porch.

OUT OF FELLOWSHIP IN PUBLIC

Fourth, this might seem a little fanatical, but if you have had a bump in the presence of others, you still need to confess right away. So what do you do if kids or other people are there? Suppose you are at a party and one of you says something (and science has also shown it is almost always the husband), and you realize with a sinking feeling that what you just said was really bad. Now what?

Most of the time, the only one who notices is the wife, and while they are out of fellowship because of what he said, nobody else notices. Once in a while, everybody does notice, and the whole room gasps. If the whole room gasps, the apology must be as public as the sin was. If you said something rude or thoughtless and everybody heard it, then correct it with everybody. Most of the time, everybody else may just be going on merrily, but the husband and wife are out of fellowship, and they don't even have to look at each other to know it. For such occasions, Nancy and I developed a hand signal for "I repent" and "You're forgiven."

It was also an ironclad rule that if the hand signal was sent, it had to be returned. You could not pretend, "Oh, ho, hum. Wonder what that was about." You may think this is kind of radical. Why not just wait until you're in the car and fix it on the way home? Because by the time you get into the car there will be fifteen other things to fix. Each offense is like a snowball rolling down a hill: each offense creates the likelihood that they will accumulate.

Agree on a surreptitious signal, catch the other person's eye, and apologize to them for what you just did, as long as it is not something that needs to be corrected with everybody. Also, the signal ought to be discrete; it should not look like you are telling her to steal third.

LEARNING TO DANCE

Finally, if you start applying these things and your spouse sees it, they may say, "You're just doing this because of that book you read. You don't mean it!" Well, when it comes to confessing sin, worse things have happened than doing so because you read about it in a book.

When you are first learning to dance, you are not really dancing. You are counting 1-2-3, 1-2-3. When you first start keeping short accounts, it is going to feel cumbersome, clunky, and artificial, apologizing as if you were doing a paint-by-numbers kit. But if you do it, and you get in the habit of doing it, you will find yourself with a tidy living room and you are going to find yourself living in a place where people want to be. Your spouse will want to be with you, and you will want to be with them. Why? Because this is harmonious. It is a livable space. We can sit down. We are not having to find the couch before we sit on it.

These are not the rules that nice people follow. They are just simple reminders to do what we should always be doing. Remember that apart from Jesus Christ, there is no way to pick up after yourself. He is the third party in your marriage relationship, and do not treat Him as an abstract principle. What do you want the aroma of your home to be? You want people to walk in and feel like Christ is there, and that Christ is there because He died on the cross and His righteousness was given to you. Christ is our teacher, and He is there admonishing and correcting, helping you as you pick these things up so that you can stand to be where you live with the people you love.

Without Christ it is hopeless. But in Christ it is mandatory, in the way breathing oxygen is necessary. Breathing is necessary if God has quickened you into life. It is mandatory only if you want to live under the blessing of Jesus.

PART 3

DECLUTTERING YOUR MARRIAGE CHECKLIST

- ❑ Do you have a pile of clutter anywhere in your house? Is it overwhelming you and keeping you from cleaning it up? Do you have any overwhelmingly "cluttered" relationships?

- ❑ What does it mean to be in a "spiritual" frame of mind? What are the reasons you correct those around you?

- ❑ Do you correct your kids for their sake? What about co-workers? Is there anybody you regularly clash with? Have you ever shut up because you knew you were not in the right mood to correct somebody?

- ❑ Do have a competitive mentality in your marriage or toward some of your friends? Is there another Christian whom you think you always need to beat?

- ❑ Do you have a grudge against anyone or even just a list of sins they have done in the back of your head?

- Do you say "You always" or "You never" to your spouse or your kids or your friends? Ask your spouse, kids, or friends if you are uncertain.

- Can you honestly say, before the Lord, that you have considered the possibility that you are part of the problem?

- Do you think of pride as the root of your other sins? Is it hard or incredibly unpleasant to confess your sins to other people?

- What do you think are your greatest virtues? Do other people like your righteous indignation, decisive leadership, maternal concern, or theological precision as much as you do? Or are they irritated? Or do they find it funny and quirky?

- Do you see yourself as the hero in your own story? Do you run through scenarios in your head in which "you showed them"?

- Do you plead the dictionary? Does your spouse often have to figure out what you mean from the subtext? Do you carefully explain back what your spouse says each time you are having a difficult conversation?

- Have you ever been brave and asked your friends if the way you raise your eyebrows or your tone of voice has become a source of irritation to them? Have you ever recorded yourself just to hear how you sound and see how you look? (Be especially careful with this.)

- Does the atmosphere in your home overflow with grace? Or are people tense and quiet?

- Do you confess your sins right away? What happens when you do not? Have you ever tried to "make up" for it with the other person by being nice instead of confessing?

- Do you clean up messes right away at your house? Do you confess sin right away?

- Do you have clear and well-defined table manners that everybody understands? Do you use manner-policing as an opportunity to criticize each other?

- Have you ever used a confession of sin as a way of getting someone else to apologize? Do you apologize as if you were the only person who was at fault? Do you include excuses, mitigating circumstances, or euphemisms to avoid making yourself look bad?

- Have you ever had a horrible argument over something that seemed ridiculously petty or small? Do you think that was the only thing at issue at the time?

- When was the last time that you remember getting out of fellowship with your wife? Did you confess right away?

- When was the last time you got out of fellowship when people were around? What did you do? If you could not confess right away, did it poison everything until you could get in private again? Have you ever confessed a clearly public sin in private?

- Did doing anything on this list feel awkward? If so, is that a problem?

www.ingramcontent.com/pod-product-compliance
Lightning Source LLC
Chambersburg PA
CBHW070453050426
42450CB00012B/3254